Contents

KU-506-935

		Page
1	The Birth of a Legend	1
2	Forest	5
3	Keano	9
4	Manchester United 1	12
5	World Cup USA	15
6	Manchester United 2	18
7	Keano Says	22
8	The Man	23
9	Keano Quiz	26

REAL LIVES

Roy Keane

Andy Croft

Published in association with The Basic Skills Agency

Hodder & Stoughton
A MEMBER OF THE HODDER HEADLINE GROUP

Acknowledgements
Cover: © Neal Simpson/EMPICS.

Photos: p. 3 © Tony Harris/PA Photos; p. 7 © Phil O'Brien/EMPICS; p. 11 © Shaun Botterill/Getty Images; p. 15 © David Cannon/Allsport; p. 18 © Laurence Griffiths/EMPICS; p. 21 © Magi Haroun/EMPICS; p. 24 © Clive Brunskill/Getty Images.

Orders: please contact Bookpoint Ltd, 130 Milton Park, Abingdon, Oxon OX14 4SB. Telephone (44) 01235 827720, Fax: (44) 01235 400454. Lines are open from 9.00–6.00, Monday to Saturday, with a 24 hour message answering service. You can also order through our website www.hodderheadline.co.uk

British Library Cataloguing in Publication Data
A catalogue record for this title is available from the British Library

ISBN 0 340 87658 5

First published 2003
Impression number   10 9 8 7 6 5 4 3 2 1
Year   2007 2206 2005 2004 2003

Typeset by SX Composing DTP, Rayleigh, Essex.
Printed in Great Britain for Hodder & Stoughton Educational, a division of Hodder Headline, 338 Euston Road, London NW1 3BH by Bath Press Ltd, Bath.

1 The Birth of a Legend

Roy Maurice Keane
was born on 10 August 1971
in the city of Cork
in the Irish Republic.

He was the fourth of five children.
They were a football-mad family.
The rest of the family
supported Manchester United.
Roy supported Spurs.

Roy Keane went to St John's Primary School
and Mayfield Community School.

He played football all the time.
Before school, at dinnertime,
after school, every weekend.
Because he was small for his age,
he only played twice for his junior school team.

He joined a local junior team when he was nine.
They were called Rockmount AFC.
He played for the Under-10s,
the Under-11s and the Under-12s.
And he was still only nine!
At the end of his first season,
Rockmount voted Roy Keane Player of the Year.
Rockmount won the League and Cup double
for the next six seasons.
They won every game for four years!

Roy Keane.

Because he was small,
Roy Keane tried to build up his strength.
He tried Gaelic football,
a game played mainly in Ireland.
He even tried boxing.

Roy Keane left school at fifteen.
He just wanted to play football.
He wrote to English league clubs asking for a trial.
No one was interested.
They all thought he was too small.
He didn't even bother writing to
Manchester United.
He thought they were too good for him!

2 Forest

When Roy was seventeen
he joined a local team
called Cobh Ramblers.
A scout from Nottingham Forest
soon spotted him playing for them.
Forest asked him to go for a trial for the club.

The Forest manager
was the famous Brian Clough.
He knew Roy Keane was special.
Forest bought him for £47,000
in May 1990.

At first Roy was homesick.
He missed his family back in Ireland.
Clough always called him the Irishman.

He played in an Under-21 competition in Holland
and scored two goals.
Soon he was in the Forest reserve team.
He scored two goals in his first game.

A few weeks later
he was in the first team against Liverpool.
In the next match,
he made a goal against Southampton.
Brian Clough was so pleased
that he kissed him in front of all the fans!
He scored his first league goal for Forest
against Sheffield United.

Keane receives the Barclay's Young Player of the
Month award at Nottingham Forest, 1991.

Roy Keane played 49 games for Forest
in his first season.
In 1991, he helped them reach
the FA Cup Final,
but they lost to Spurs.
The team he'd supported as a boy.

The next season he scored against Spurs
to take Forest to the League Cup Final.
They lost 1–0 to Manchester United in the final.
He was voted Young Eagle of the Year
and Player of the Year at Forest.

In three seasons at Nottingham Forest,
Roy Keane played 153 games.

Keano

Roy Keane is a very special player.
He doesn't score many goals.
He doesn't dribble.
He doesn't cross the ball.
But he's one of the best midfield players
in the world.

He may be small,
but he wins the ball.
He tackles hard.
He isn't afraid.
He passes well.

He jumps high.
He can head the ball.
He makes goals.
He makes late runs into the box
and scores important goals.
He runs and runs
and runs and runs
and never stops.

Roy Keane never gives up.
Roy Keane wants to win.

This also means he gets a lot of injuries.
It means he sometimes gets in trouble with referees.

Roy Keane in action at Old Trafford, 2002.

4 Manchester United 1

At the end of 1992–3, Forest were relegated.
Manchester United wanted to buy Roy Keane.
So did Arsenal and Blackburn.
United manager Alex Ferguson
had already tried to buy him twice.
This time Ferguson got his man.

In July 1993, Roy Keane
joined Manchester United
for £3.75 million.
It was a British record.
And he was still only 21 years old.

Keane played his first game for United
in the Charity Shield
against Arsenal.
In his first league game,
he crossed the ball for Ryan Giggs to score.
In his first game at Old Trafford,
United's home ground,
he scored two goals against Sheffield United.
A few weeks later,
he scored two goals in the Champions' League.

In the 1992–3 season, Roy Keane helped United
win the FA Cup and League 'Double'.
They had never won both in the same season.

Manchester United celebrate a goal in the
1994 FA Cup Final.

5 World Cup USA

Roy Keane was soon a regular in the Ireland team.

He first played for Ireland
in 1991 against Chile.
In 1994, he helped his home country
reach the World Cup
in the USA.

Ireland beat Italy 1–0.
They lost 1–2 to Mexico.
They drew 0–0 with Norway.
They drew 0–0 with Holland.
Then they were out of the World Cup.

Roy Keane wasn't happy.
He didn't like Ireland's tactics.
The Ireland manager, Jack Charlton
told the players to kick the ball up the pitch.
Roy Keane didn't want to.
He wanted to play a passing game.

Keane was far from happy.
But he was still voted
the best Irish player in the World Cup.

Keane and Eric Cantona celebrate winning the
Double in 1996.

6 Manchester United 2

In 1996, United won the Double again.
When Eric Cantona retired in 1997
Roy Keane became United captain.

He missed the 1997–8 season
because of a knee injury.
United won nothing that year.

When he came back from injury,
United won the Double again in 1999.
Only three other players in history
have won both the League and FA Cup
three times.

Manchester United were the best team in Britain.
Roy Keane wanted them
to be the best team in Europe.
In 1998, he took them to the
Champions' League final.
He scored in the semi-final
against Juventus.
United went on to beat Bayern Munich
in the final.
Roy Keane couldn't play in the match
because he had a yellow card.
He was banned from playing.

In 1999, he was voted
Manchester United Player of the Year.

In 2000, United were champions again.
And again in 2001.
Roy Keane has helped United
win the League six times.

In nine seasons,
Roy Keane has played
376 games for Manchester United
and scored 46 goals.

In 2000, he was voted FA Player of the Year.
In 2001, United fans voted him
seventh best United player in history.
Alex Ferguson has said Keane is perhaps
the best United player of all time.

Roy Keane holding the trophy for FA Player of the Year 1998–1999 with
Sandy Busby (son of Sir Matt Busby).

7 Keano Says

The following are quotes from Roy Keane himself.

I love winning.
I would be just as happy without my money.
Roy Keane is not a great player.
The only thing that goes with the flow
is dead fish.
It is the lows that keep me going.
Players need to stand up and be counted.
Good players don't necessarily make good teams.
Work as hard as you can and eventually
you will get your rewards.
There are so many players better than me
who haven't made it.
Getting to major finals is what it is all about.
Fail to prepare, prepare to fail.
Some people are sheep. I am a wolf.

8 The Man

Roy Keane is one of the most famous
footballers in the world.
He is captain of the most famous
football club in the world.

He has played 56 times for his country.
He is the highest paid player at Old Trafford.
He is recognised everywhere he goes.
United fans love Keano.

Keano: popular with the fans!

He may be a football 'hard man',
but Roy Keane is also a very private person.
Roy Keane does a lot of work for charity.
He is a quiet, shy man.
He likes staying at home with his family.

Is he a hard man
or a family man?
Is he a saint or a sinner?
One thing is certain:
Roy Keane is a winner,
and a fantastic football player.

9 Keano Quiz

1 In which country was Roy Keane born?

2 What other sports did Roy Keane play as a boy?

3 Which team did Roy Keane support
   when he was a boy ?

4 How much did Nottingham Forest pay for
   Roy Keane?

5 Against which country did Roy Keane
   win his first cap for Ireland?

6 How many games did Roy Keane play for
   Nottingham Forest?

7 How much money did Manchester United pay
   for Roy Keane?

8 How many times has Roy Keane
   won the Premiership?

9 How many times has Roy Keane won the
   Double?

10 Against which club did Roy Keane score his
    first goal for Manchester United?